TURQUOISE DOOR

FINDING MABEL DODGE LUHAN IN NEW MEXICO

Also By Lauren Camp

This Business of Wisdom

The Dailiness

One Hundred Hungers

TURQUOISE DOOR

FINDING MABEL DODGE LUHAN IN NEW MEXICO

POEMS

LAUREN CAMP

3

THREE: A TAOS PRESS

First U.S. edition 2018

Book Design & Typesetting: Lesley Cox, FEEL Design Associates, Taos, NM
Press Logo Design: William Watson, Castro Watson, New York, NY
Front Cover Artwork: Emil Bisttram, *Sublimation, 1963*, Private Collection,
Denver, Colorado
Author Photograph: Bob Godwin, Santa Fe, NM

Text Typeset in Gotham

Printed in the United States of America by Cottrell Printing Company

ISBN: 978-0-9972011-9-2

THREE: A TAOS PRESS
P.O. Box 370627
Denver, CO 80237
www.3taospress.com

10 9 8 7 6 5 4 3 2 1

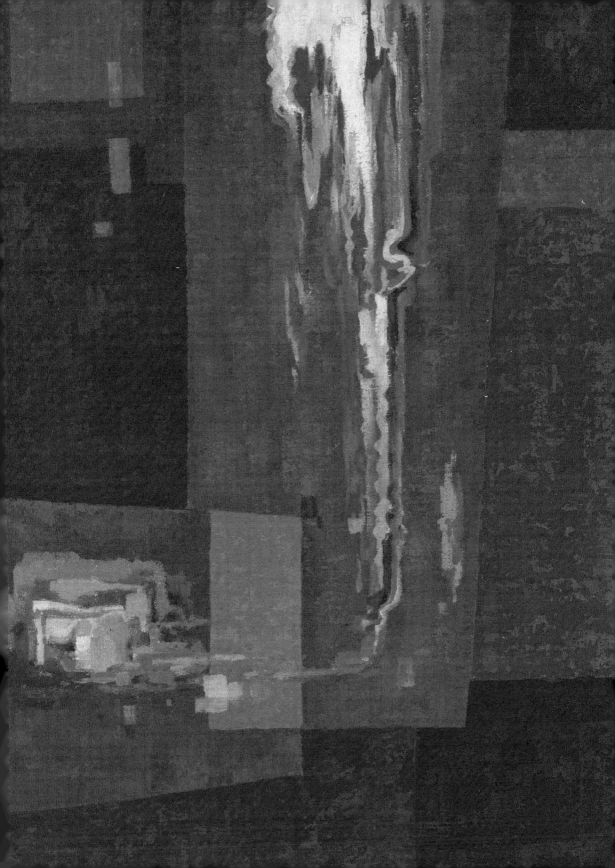

CONTENTS

— Choosing an Archetype for Mabel Dodge Luhan

— The Fine Mist of Buzzing

...the whole world comes to Mabel's.

—GEORGIA O'KEEFFE TO ALFRED STIEGLITZ, MAY 1929

Our Beginning and Our End

But for rooms of reminders, to survive we flee through aching skin
of unrepentant light and drifting ember to the filter of timber

spilled further, the earth moving its pathways with farmers
and the very slow lament of dusty colorful graves beside each blue curve

on each road. Conjuring direction depends on how violet
the sun, depends on how far we want to map to a new mountain.

We must become less injured. Go through tired trees past *the drink water place*
and *the dry spotted place*—both deserter and victim. Leave behind

the place people hurled stones. Because escape is a wound,
stay to the soil less shallow, less starved. At *the round earth*

drive through *the village of good obsidian*, past the proud
church, past heaps of lurking desperation,

crutches and dirt. Along rinds of rivers unscrolling
to small liquid ribbons embroidered with crownsbeard and artifacts,

past places that peak. Places chiseled with trivial codes
of what once was whole. See what you see growing flexible.

Heights, sooner than later. Settle to *Taa-, the place of red willow*,
of Mabel, of thick dwellings. The pulp of water

picking small holes in the ground. Leaving home, let go the fists
of many empty blossoms, the cinder. All the crusts of fields. Every road

comes to an end and then bends, and out of this the steady is made,
offering proof that the thin far away gives a name to place

the calm, the place before passing through, the place
around confession, a longer pause to linger. With every place

become the gap, and greet the bats and worms,
the rocks, the taut horizon, repeat all praise for spots of green.

Raw, Interrupted

First Longing

This morning I drove off to forget
the lines of crow, the clot of burning
smog, the double-sided
                    fire-light: its mislaid desire. No more
        talk about the carpet of wanting

a life not clasped in ash. Already,
I'm collecting ghosts on the bricks
        of a different patio. Don't you wish
                    you could be here? Right now,
        where you are, helicopters

have been crossing, leaving white tracks
in the tide of sky. I will forget the sky
        with reddened gesture, glad to be not altered
                    by each twitched wind. I'll go
        about sleeping, or setting up my prayers. Merely
this—a guttural hope

for what's meant for me. You understand
                    I had to cross from our home
        where we could see the dying
anywhere we stood. *Come, rain…*
                    we said at every corner: *come finish*

what's been started. My love, I felt each slash
                    and lapse of summer's sudden anger,
and made a choice to leave you with it
        for these weeks. I couldn't manage
                    where it burns the branch,

the strand, the habitat: land-blind
to leaf and skin. I needed a throat of air:
        or no, I *wanted* it.

ACRE TO MOLECULE

Goodbye each sleepless night
on pale cotton, each choking.

I'm not ashamed to retreat to a cottage hunched over
a forgotten road—

For two days I still see what was

as time returns to seconds
amid the simple shape of unmemorable houses. I leave
the land to its sweat, and the world

might go on melting. Right now, I want to see the molecule,
forget those acres.

LETTER TO MABEL: UNDER VIGAS

Yes, it is true, I left what was flammable. My house with keyholes, my reliance on grievance. Left day and night in fire-pirouette, the scratched blackening, the brittle mountain heat escaping containment.

I was afraid for the inevitable trees, half-dressed in flames, afraid of the casting wind and its awful crooning.

When I stepped up to your house, all atmosphere and architecture, wet with understandings, how soft I felt. The need for resolution was rinsed of its spears.

Am I here to recover, breeze by blue breeze? It sounds as if my life were all darkness. There were details. Home was ritual. The birds were numinous. Here, light roams around windows, offering two sides of praises, unfinished.

DEAR ONE WHO STAYS

I have gone away before
          even while I slept by your side. I've laced other

fingers, drank another man's
          thoughts from multiple tables, four beds.

Then, I lingered. I'm sorry. I was mistaking my heart
          through the junipers. For months

no pen took to its subject without blackening
          the weft of the paper. I had the expense

of my memory and you let me spend it
          far into debt. Our life was range

and its stresses. Back then, we listened to the sharp
          tongues of finches, the sheets as they twisted, the side door

with its finish. I've already shown you I won't stay away.
          I've truthed out the dangers.

THE HOUSE OF WHAT WE INVENT

The Big House was built and old stones
carried in strangers, who brought their horizons

and stretched them to extravagant rising
language. Even in the 1920's, every visitor

was temporary if not left for hours
to their papers and actions. Leaning into their silence

may not have been pleasure but how
they survived. All this in my mind as I roam

from my typing to talk, ever wrapped in my longing
for supple statements. A hundred years on and the heartbeat

and whistle of detail, and the scorn
of such detail—the wrist keeps composing

its phrases. When we're sharpening
our roused vowels, we see only

syntactical constellations and trials.
Some nights when my love asks me for love, I want to answer

in song, but must first check the locks
on my language, and choose scribbles

of fingers and tongue, rather than text again speaking
its impossible clauses. One need

for another. And so I suppose the geniuses
might have stood by the hearth and heard not the crackle

of burning branches, nor the victories and voices
of others, but only words

wound in their hearts, only rhythms
they hadn't yet figured. Even in parlor they continued

to whittle raw sentences, to gather the plausible haze
into meaning—the brave instant of story,

caesura, stresses and order. Each mind holds
what fits it, and the breath and the consonants.

The hand pens its geography.
No one would choose this constant fire.

Past Tense

When I first stepped through
this doorway, my arms heavy with past tenses,

I could still hear almost
         everything else in my life:
                  the choreography of desiccated passions,
                  daybreak weeping
         by fractions. Even the moonlight
hadn't left me behind.

Everywhere, blue
         pressed down to blue. The color left its moods
                  by my ears.

Summer Drifting in Shy Talk

I thought to walk by pine and sage
to a river bed (all dry, of course). Thankful for a breeze
in leaves, I sat beside a yarrow crop.

I sat as ants rushed back
and forth, and sometimes talked. I walked
and walked along the rocks around the back

to grass and past the aspen, past
the house, past the first of early clouds
already turning mauve. The hush that came

was mine, inside. I heard the wind and honks,
and folks off to the east. I heard the dark
descend by notes, and then an anxious bird.

I stood until another bird crossed by to claim
the first. I heard them chitter, heard one soothe.
The psalms of night revolved.

Dear Mabel,

Of course the extraordinary found you here, in the subtraction between church and ditch. In the shards of each hour, translucent light. Tony's voice, drifting, feathered. I wish I could have heard it. Tony in hides tanned with deer brains and liver. The sum of your walks, those rhythmic circles below the mountain.

After the third costume of monogamy, you gave in to the clothes of the desert. Evenings beneath bleached vigas.

Each morning you depended on pigeons with their textured secrets, their dancing, and in the kitchen, men eating hanks and pulp, their large swallows. You lived within people, by stones. Bathed inside glass. In Lawrence's prudence. Finally, satisfied.

Already, you have become my mind.

Late afternoon, I sit beneath trebled trees in the patient day, the sky sharply demarcated: white to blue. Nothing to notice but the slope of my back in the seat in the shade, the chokecherry bush in rapture. Church bells shake, all ellipses. How often is this possible—a cleaned-out time made long?

Clouds merge, become my continent. What yesterday, what tomorrow in this white wooden chair. An anonymous portion of safety. This nature, much as the hate and hurt and dirt.

The windows of the solarium open out. Now, and nest. The birds at ease, the fall of ordinary air. A stem, some toothsome leaves with holes. Some resting.

RAINBOW ROOM AND THE RED CHAIR

I am granted every fork,
every chair, every blossom,
the lantern and saffron, escape
or alliance. It's an agreement I made:
to spell the spare creaks, to carry
many books and not anyone else.
Hard work to stretch to the spines,
to rattle out commas. To become the woman
who nibbles on bacon and sits
where light swings to lift out
each line, putting a final yes
at the bottom. I wanted a bathtub,
but I am paraphrasing the particular
into what I would not use.
All I really needed were clauses
and some evenings, I walk
to the plaza where burred people
dance. Much has been offered.
Pink lands on umber.
Extravagant light hollers into my silence.
I am hiding in public with my definition
of the spectrum of stars
arranged exactly as frames
for my pictures. And again, when I can,
my body in the thicket

of upholstery, only rising for corn cakes
and scones. I spend more hours
by the abiding lamp, black pen
in hand. I always intend a stop
to absorption. Room to room,
the seclusion is mercy.
The skin of my husband is distant.
Every night is desire
for summer grasses. After a while,
I find less in first times. Again,
the next day, I lift myself out
of the red heart in the corner near the low-
lying windows, and announce
to the flowers nothing is wrong.
I'm looking for quiver, and will accept
only a corolla of words. They open their faces,
unblinking. I cling to their attention.

LETTER TO MABEL: LINGERING IN THE CORNER

I am obliged to measure a variation of phrases by my pen at the paper—
in this room where you gathered and broke your memory to pages.
Another palmful of berries, the delicate skin of a whole afternoon.

Many times I've repeated my name to strangers, each syllable a pressure
on my tongue. They reply with sounds that seem dusted, with primary and
secondary laughter. We only say who we've been somewhere else in the
world, in those other houses, other temperatures. We only back and forth
and *thank you* and *after all*. No disclosing the truth.

All their speech inside me: jagged and ripe. In response, I have learned to
ask for excuse from the clamor. To understand instead the open door
shrugged with sun. To chew on my voice alone by the lamp. Along the
portal, another stone splits. The register of words vanishes in branches.

Between Answers
and Branches

FEATHERS AND MOUNTAIN

In the upstairs low bedroom
       with its odorless space: walls
and cracks asking
       back, Tony wrote
plumage. His large hands caused birds
       in all corners,
in ridges, dabbed grace
       in tangible places. He stood

       slow on the overhung
porch in wool blanket where
       layers of stars
etched into sky. No
       objective. He nodded, patient,
accruing the heaven, its noises. Sky despaired
       of color, this land
at the rim of the pueblo

noosed now
       by winter. Each night,
he turned again
       to feathers and wing, everything
familiar. In the distance, long count
       of hills, horse hair,
blood. He looked down
       the balcony to tanagers

       and magpies mistaking
the dawn. He knew
       the cartilage of the house, the heavy
physical body of silence. Tony kept standing
       still, kept picturing
birds lift from his large hands
       to the rooms, then only the wind
as it slid down the mountain.

What Needed Saying

This house never had a complete pause. It was written
     all over with noises
and symptoms, articulated language.

     By evening, the moon extracts the crisp skin
from the sky. The slight staircase wavers.

     A truncated door borders the kitchen,
its turquoise triangles, milkweed and roots.

     This house understands
the doves double mourning through summer,
     and the stay and momentum

when there's room to unfasten, but after some years,
     the house wouldn't offer its favors.

The moon laid its face on those slabs of stone
     where I walk between dark and ground,
between answers and branches.

THE SIGHING OF THE KIT CARSON CEMETERY

On my way into town, in a hurry, in a hat,
I pass the cemetery. The sun is brimming

with piled-on heat. I enter into the buried, the bandits.
Around me, names extracted from books.
I have stopped going to town, and now I am standing

under the eternal body of sky
in an architecture of mountains in territory

deepened with weeds. Nothing trembling.
In the park amphitheater, women drum and dance,
raising hands as if measuring elevation. As if they see

past ravens, past leaves interlocked to cottonwood tops,
see over clouds. I step, no longer elsewhere,

but etched in the graveyard. At the back corner,
a lumped stone and a low altar. And still the throat
of the drum. On Mabel's diminutive grave,

synthetic petals, all purple, some pinecones, a dingy
lace doily, a button, a dime,

a necklace (—no, two, or three), and pieces of glass,
a bottlecap, whatever is human, available.
Someone's slightly curled painting.

I re-home next to her bones. The music continues: tassels
and boots, some stomping. Sitting like this

on the ground, under the mutable smell
of locust and desert, I am taller than the small
monument. Also on the altar, a dried thistle, thorny.

Women pace a circle, turn around. The drum releases
its wisdom. Mabel's in the corner, in the morning,

the evening, forever, the grass shaggy and limp
beside her. Wires cross wires in loops as a fence.
The air is a blanket tinted four ways,

then reversed. Now the women are chanting.
Beats lift out of ashes. They're not very good,

but I like their wide distension
resting on history. Where I am, no one exhales,
and I haven't said a word, but I believe

she is grateful for a salon again,
for someone to need her. When I rise, the sun flattens

its feathers on ground. On my way out, I notice
double hollyhocks, pink and inevitably alert,
looking both ways, as if responding to many questions.

GOD OF THE CLUSTERED NIGHT

Juniper berries are little prayers

or small ghosts

or blue sacks
that settle
like dust in our throats.

Under the house with no roof
people dance
in numb light.

Where bones chafe against dirt
others walk on fire
in circles of knowledge.

People crowd in with dissonant blankets
in the posture
of each other's heartbeat.

Wind-churning sage
mixes with mercury
arsenic
rusted metal.

Desert clouds plump
then conjugate
all the pleasure for hours.

We avoid the cemetery
or go toward

its fragments of fossils
and wings strewn toward dark.

Let more coyotes walk us in—
guard the last disappointment.

WILLA CATHER AT THE BIG HOUSE

*Elsewhere the sky is the roof of the world; but here
the earth was the floor of the sky.*

—WILLA CATHER

Every day, a topic. An index of emotion.

Every day, the old contours and preoccupation
with adornment. Every day, the fever

unknown, and the coiling whisper,
a flick and bend of the violet alphabet:

more how than strict.
A simple line—she keeps tearing it apart.

The project is practical.
She starts to wake early to hear

the white of her fist over hours
and days, the anatomy of attention

which tells her
Go in another direction. Always

an occasional underline.
This is the door to a few years with its gaps.

This is the skin of her breathing.
She sings each time she troubles.

The line again: so peevish.

And so, it is given, her allegiance.

LETTER FROM MABEL: THE HALF MEASURE TO PLEASURE AND PHRASES

How I craved a muse that couldn't escape, that would wake
to the dust-blaze of letters. I invited

compassion and had instead the heavy edges
of friends with their dark reactions. Maybe that's not right.

I had what I wanted—gardens,
the salted long walls, the invention

of fragments and titles, a buttress,
brocade. As a girl I licked wallpaper

so the flocked roses could touch me. Every guest
was a dreamer. I gave each a bed. Night

clenched us, and Lawrence's strange stories leaked
into the sitting room where they kept me

unending. I preferred the opposite
side of the puritan center. I was ruthless, but breaking—

or broken on the lip of each interaction. I spanned the closed
doors, the tables, the margins. I made a room

of each memory. And another, another. Filled with my icons:
our amateur gods—their stories

and verses. Each evening, I climbed stairs
to see Pueblo land penetrate into refraction.

The light couldn't say what it saw. The town practiced
squinting, called Tony *savage*,

and me. So we married. A life begun in landscape
flecked with ravens. Now crowds

of tourists gather under a sky that has stayed
at the windows. They can't stop talking, waving their hands.

What do they know, scavenging my details?
They can buy all the tomahawks

they please; they'll still be drifting in my front door.
Each night, I'll glide past, shaking my skirts.

Canyon Trail #59

Let me green every turn toward aspen.
Let me move, always seeing
the scarred and prophetic.
Let me believe in vulnerable sprouting,
and learn verses of water
in alluvial soil. And then dream
that versions of fragile
can somehow reverse.
This isn't a litany
with no reason. Life wants
another morning, wants to feed
on the prosperous mountain,
to enumerate roots again, to peak
off the grief. Let us each begin
fresh with attention. Let us see
succulence, the casual desert. Let us be
less anxious each time
the trees shuffle. Over years
of Julys, we have learned
to expect wreckage in mountains.
Now I learn to lean low to sweet roses
to count whatever is rising,
to follow whatever is recently back.

TO WAKE AT THE POINT OF ALL SLEEPING

Then, everything slept.
                    —LARRY LEVIS

The small roads of the town were sleeping, and the main road
slept, too, very tired. The trees were sleeping and the cedar
and the many hard-hearted, hued and carved doors.
Traffic lights slept in their green enclosures,
and houses were sleeping, and fences and trailers.
On the road to the bridge, a graveyard of junk cars slept
in their awkward spaces and pauses. And the strange scrub
that made fields—that scrub slept, crinkled, though the cows
were awake, just not moving. Garbage trucks drooped together
in a lot, fatherly, motherly, gentle, with their mouths closed,
virescent and utterly silent. And at that time of day, that certain
time, clouds puckered, or pillowed, communal.
Mile markers were sleeping, and the landfill and lounges,
the billboards, the laundromat, the church bells and organ.
The mountains were sleeping in their blue sheets of haze,
and because I didn't know Tiwa for mountain, I kept repeating,
The mountains, even the mountains have not yet awoken!
The sun was still sleeping on the floor of the earth, and the moon
wasn't there, so was probably snoozing nearby,
but in the gorge, water began stirring. One bird advanced
five short calls, then another, much longer, that whippered
through me, a song for the morning in case anyone was waking.
That composition revived other birds, and they raced
round the canyon, exclaiming, and buoyed.
Already, so quickly, I could hear cars rumble, offended
by daylight. The rising hadn't been rosy or succulent, chewable,
sparked—but all of a sudden. The sun not yet at 7AM was full
white in the sky. A plane crossed the gorge and lifted,
then circled to see it again: that big gash beneath us, the steep carve
of canyon, the shear in this rock. Now, everything was rising
in the specific distance, everything was energy, flare;
the noise was consuming, everything angled with light.

Icon

I pass roses beside fallen rock, their petals in crescents.
The river stays quiet
though versions of water continue.
Context is holy: the slow beam of light pure with deer limbs.
A stone walk wends behind trees and weary leaves.
Four magpies at the sprinkler,
black beaks filled with capture.
When I walk into the Big House, the door ajar,
a Welsh man with a half-smile offers a beer.
We look across Pueblo land at lowered eyebrows of light.
Other people close the door.
"I'd like to leave it all behind. Not go back, you know?"
I do not respond.
On the path, gold hearts of forsythia open.
The sky is only sky, not endless silenced trees.
Not insistent hues and curls of soot.

HERE, AND HERE

Been here
a while, and I haven't yet

read all
different ways the beginning—

Life is part thus,
and part commonplace:

the rippling light
riding the edge of the porch

and so what
if the ditch ends

in rust and abrupt
obsidian? We see it all, and take

pictures of elevation,
unable to find another view. We love

the detachment, the broken
lock

on the window.
To whom should we rejoice

about what
never happens?

AWAKE ALL NIGHT. NOT

to tooth, to mistake
oneself. Awake to keep the after-

taste of falling down. Of
what is argued. To keep
the rain as destination. To hear

night pulped, to see parched stars stir
in shadow. To feel one's skin
on backwards.

Each Journey
a Chapel

HERETIC

Without purpose, I drive up a new mountain,
not the familiar Sangre de Cristos—blood

of Christ—with their permanent reason
and praises I see from my true bedroom window.

I drawl past cabins of sleepy habits,
the geometry of windows, a tangle of streets

neither fast nor direct. My eyes travel to cedar
and the sumac's coarse branches.

Wild-rose breath bursts at the shoulder.
Give it here, such beauty. I'd fall for each

coral center—and the aspen arms
with their thin, gauzy shaking. Somewhere

between pine are the wide eyes of a God
I never found in any place of worship,

not even when I sat on the velvet and held
the prayer book. I have chosen my faith.

Give me the chapel of elk in the distance
because all roads have thistles.

VANISHING POINT

The Couse-Sharp Historic Site, Taos, New Mexico

1

—wherever they pointed, I
hovered, intending to uncommon the vigas
and the artist's thick-oil render
            of the calves and warm shoulders of Native men
looking off, perhaps noble

or just exposed—

                To secure details, I also snapped
                quick shots of brushes
        and beakers, and the three libraries with spines
        of gray books on explosives, Poe's
                        poems

and kinematics hedged
in infinite defensible order.

                The slight couple (leftover
        family) stirred through
        and lengthened my limited history
                        of Paris salons and the Taos
                        Society, offering dates all the while

        like a calendar: *19-2*
        and *19-6*, those buttoned-back years
                        returning a century, blurring.
        My mind tried turning

each habit of light to luxurious finish, wanting firm
        lines to come proud
    from my palm. The three of us
           edged the porch as rain painted
               its few evanescent

    drops on a horizon weighted
    with eaves. The woman again pointed. I noticed
           the delphiniums with their blue
        wings were the same
              larkspur that grew

    in a sepia photo framed in black in the office.

2

—at every bend,
 I fastened to the carved
        doors, the cracked
    wall that carried true
           years (though he said
    in his twisted
        voice they'd likely
        repair it, *So rotted
through*). In the garage, old fog
    through each window.

3

—room to room, the elders,
        in whispers, freed what keeps
        moving

            backward. Beaded moccasins lay
                flexed in a trunk.
                I kept looking at what hadn't

                escaped. The green creeper
                      in the garden was clasping
                      and growing.

4

—each turn, I faced gazes
        that limn dim rooms. Wherever they pointed,

            life was reversed from
            a farewell to a found.

The walls were still strong to the inmost.
        All day, I arced through
        the points of losing,
            ending last
            in the room lost most

                to time. A clock stood
        in pursuit
        of minutes, or arms.
                It couldn't be wound. One last
                    slow calculation.

Temple of Lawrence

On the road up, a right, and a right. I follow
Keep Out signs, expecting human clamors

and ripening. Clouds firmly say Enter,
Persevere! In those days, he was only a man,

and he needed medicine. His skin took in
the clear air. Sentences hardened and were swallowed,

defied. The house nearly permeable
nuzzles O'Keeffe's immense ponderosa

with its aura of needles. Lawrence's words fell on desert—
minimal, worn. Finger, ink, a furious wind. Nothing spotless.

...all these great, dynamic words were half dead now
or maybe more living, landscaped

before the actual dying. The ranch has lapsed
into drought. Such a plain day, unwrapped and refracted.

Sharp-elbowed sun. At the shrine, in the concrete,
the now silent body. In the cool room, inverted

hard-dot hemispheres painted an overzealous
yolk-yellow. Those walls cry out, high-keyed,

gleaming, unchaste. What in this periphery
is precisely remembered? What is written, repressed?

On the return, I pass through a gesture
of downed cottonwoods and appraise *the strange gods*

once more. The caretaker latches the gate after me.
Everything folded up, closed. But the road is ready to take me

to the curve of the loins of the mountains, such a vast opening
of light, the view an involuntary demand on the eye

...helplessly desirous...the intense movement...
the warm soft body of clouds. I am euphoric—*so close.*

LETTER TO MABEL: FROM A DOOR TURNING INWARD

I drove through the old blinking light to the ranch you gave Lawrence.

As if the road could take me through reasonable perspective. The road
with its spindly bushes and dust. The sky, combed and curling.

The ranch is bending down. The body of land baked in sun. Beside his door
stands a pity of trees. Even Georgia's pine has suffered and suffered again,
and is now without fragrance, needles whipped from the heat.

Despite sudden afflicted weeds and shamble, the needy arrive for opinions.
Yet the house has shed its unsteady hand. Every breach, each final line,
the pace of his sentences. Walls in the cottage crack.

We want his spelling of sorrow, all the trembling. Have we asked too much?

Up the slight hill, where he holds to his revolutions, yellow lumps indulge
in a pattern. I nearly kneeled in its persistence, or I should say, reeled as
it billowed.

The dark grew rough, and I left. Time was again to its pauses. I saw two
horizons: one when I looked back, hunted by hawks.

GREEN LESSON

Hot breeze through old cottonwoods
today. I walk fences
by hogans facing the wrong
                                    direction. Clouds

                    in taffied circles and a few drops
of lazy rain. I look up to mountain chains

and cliffs—
sediment, erosion, shale in ochres
                    and sun-bleached sandstone. Not one

            plane, but rises
      and plateaus. Wind at the back

      of my neck. Tree limbs realign,
position the sky to alcoves. Even the dust

is familiar. Georgia's black door at her house
                              with its shadows

            of multiple heights. The rooms break apart.
            Extruded

silence. Summer

                        on its way
to pleating colors. Branches spill

            with leaves. I sit seeing green
                        at all angles. Hearing flies.

LAST STAIN OF JUNE SUN

Finally, after friable hours, the heat relaxed
       and unwound. I wandered down cobblestone,
a bend to the right, then a corner—to a street
       someone had mentioned as *pretty*,
and I strolled for a while, admiring the slow heart

of sun in a loosening composition of peaches
       and pinks with a delicate darkness, and the moon not
yet replacing it. Soon, I'd need to be where I wanted.
       But now, with trees lithe beside me, and yarrow and wire-
wrapped walls hiding courtyards, I walked past

piles of bikes and old cars. Private poverty—through mesh
       fences, tin Guadalupes, wild red roses
blooming into agreement. Looking into long cracks
       and drooping corners, I found the line
between life's tired engines. Folks talked

fats and greases on porches we call *portals*.
       I believe people here hide their need,
piñon-green and salty. I kept walking, breathing
       the stories. I felt the sun digging
furrows and took myself home in the rolling air.

THE AGNES MARTINS AT THE HARWOOD MUSEUM

She draws the lines across her canvas, lead so faint on white,
as she draws the curtains down each night, organized and quiet.

Each night she draws water for her bath, constraining
hot with cool, and sinks her aging body in, bone

to flesh to mind. She draws courage from the hope
of space and energy, and layers it in lines she draws around herself:

compassion. She draws each day from 9 to noon, an austere
attraction to the almost not there. The line holds scarcity and excess.

She pencils down her marks. She draws a crate to ship her work,
a simple cube of native pine, a box to hold the overwhelming world.

With each straight line she draws, she wavers just a bit, a breath,
her hand shaking with the discipline of drawing what we need.

She draws what I so long had missed, the divine queue of patience
and of solitude. And as I sit among her work,

I draw a breath in prayer for the mindfulness she drew.
The longer miracle of vacancy fills the room.

FIRST RAIN IN EIGHT MONTHS

Its little stammers,
a beautiful sound like an apology—
rain kisses the house, licks mortar and stucco,
keeps searching for more truths,
so we won't know any other.

This is the reward.
Smells punctuating all of the acres.
Rain repeats its flung kindnesses
to the small room all night.

Screens writhe and streak with long skins
of water. Rain recites its vows of remaining.
The burning is made into a question.

—

Rain was.
It was!

In the morning, nothing
of its rich musk—

PLUCKING THE LAKE FROM DEVOTION

The music of worship needs sometimes to echo
a body of water, the makers of breath
to be saved by unfaltering nature,
to be drawn from their traces, and travel
above to a clearing. So you might understand why
we should not be allowed to wander
into every larkspur and trail fork, why we must leave
some domains in the distance, not structure a day
with backpacks and bootprints
around someone's temple—the depth that holds
context for hope. Reality is sometimes more
myth than contours. I'm narrowing down to a specific
soil in the desert and a time older
than the sum of its parts. When water had edges
and basins and pine into distance. The version
most often repeated claims two eagle plumes
sited a pueblo on a land draped with bare places.
In dust and from dust, strong arms wrought repeating
walls and ladders to fathom the sky. Wind bent
and reshaped and vanished. The people lived
in dimensions of owl between dawn and moon. Lived hard
in their origins as cool water flowed
from the mountain. Water was favor, and they named
its crossing for fields, fire and horses. Hawks passed above
and aimed with grand movement. Around them
over time, the people saw violence—new roads, wire fences
and closure. The crowd of such disruption creased
their reason but they bent again with stone
to the corn, transferred thought back to the sparing
desert, returned up their rungs. To gather their senses
they climbed past the amber
hair of the deer through sun-glare and hills

to a lake far from the near earth
of the normal. The vessel of nothing but tears,
to each other's reflection. They went to the lake to rename
their universe, to say Not today Not
tomorrow, and to measure the cause
of their home and of regular days. At the lake ripples
choired, open-mouthed. And look, here's a danger line: the lake
belonged to the people. To catch their pleas
and whatever they do when they need
another essential beginning. The strong people
might only have needed the repentant light. Or they might
have offered their flaws or other injustice. I'll never know.
And you should never know, and that's the importance.
When I read about the lake's acquisition, I imagine
spirited flowers that spiral up
beside water. We all want to be changed
by such colors. The truth is other people were given
permission to hike the beautiful earth
and photograph its shimmers. Borrow the blue.
Tell me when do you want others in your prayers? Tell me
how a lake could be taken. The strong people took
truth as burden, but remembered standing safe
against sky when the lake was glad to see them.
Years crawled over the water without offering
this private sequential shape for wounded refrains
and invocations. A request isn't always
a solution. The people asked in languages for the extravagant
muscle of water, its many windows. They asked
its solace. They asked and asked
and with drummed cadence. For 64 years, they asked
with dented voices, shuffling vowels.
And when the lake was returned, they planted their feet
in its mist, offered it wings, bones and their endings.

Pinwheeled *Descansos*

Where many men name
a street for themselves, I lurch
the car toward
the blushing sky.
The two lanes are shifting
curves and sun-brine.
On this long afternoon,
I drive gravel scribbled
with corners where the road runs
to a banner of olive and sand,
to the middle of mountains,
the piñon vast at this elevation.
In the unanticipated gesture of bend
and swerve we'll always find bones
in pieces. I can tolerate nothing
more small and haunting
than these symbols left to spin,
their eager petals placed in the point of grief,
and whirling witless in the wind.
Another sad story turning,
irrefutable on the shoulder.
By dare or fear, we take the curled
route fast, our glances passing
these chambered vanes
and their countless greetings.
Frothed clouds hang above
where people ghost, unfinished.
The earth memorizes their forms and division,
their skids along the taut
rural ground. Over and over
we crisscross dusty light, move toward
and away. How far 'til we get there,
'til we break the surface?

LUCERO PEAK CAVE

First, a fence, then a gate.
Alone in the morning's bright imprecision,

I know when I find the cave of the woman.
Last night, Lawrence had murmured long clauses

that lined up in my head
when I should have been sleeping.

The intimate alphabet, invaluable
hours, infinite regress of endings kept

blurring my vision. Even after the clock
molded minutes thick into hours, I twisted

and meandered through
pages coated with dew. Now, flint light,

small splinters of wind. The cave is wet
in odd places: ledges, silver cavities of rock.

Many long drips of water—not together, not fast—
leave a white line in nooks.

I am alert to the upright pine against glittering aspen.
Still alert to the sentence.

Someone would die here without anyone saying
a word. The sky lays down blue, with gray in its center,

and fingered with madness. Overhead
the same sun, no longer tender.

I have never before climbed into a paragraph,
or a conclusion. Leaving the site, I read

summer's flat light on the road.
The sun is unpunctuated but reveals its opinions.

HOUR OF THE TURNING MOON

junipers line up

by loose-limbed
cottonwoods

sky fades to large
remnants
of blue

every porch light
twinkles

at the time of night
when details
haze

and without
wind
the mountains
hunker

and sit
soaked
in tinctures of pink

Rigorous Grays

THE FIRST TO REFUSE

A dubious week, and what remains
is more empty

of understanding. We were in the careful
room, exhausting the pretty.

The man thanked me
for not kissing him. Less

to carry back. His speech
was in tune and somewhat

restrictive. We stood
in the house without flowers

without segment. With somewhere
his wife and children—

but here, with only the light
cloth of summer. We stood

in our bodies,
awkward. There were analogous doors

that went away
from me. No one knocked.

This was after he paid
for dinner. We'd sat on the porch,

four of us, with improbable voices.
His sister-in-law smoked

as I shivered. She loaned me
her cardigan. Later,

he walked me through
all the rocky

places to my small room.
I count my defiance in the unknown

spice of his sternum.
By myself, when he left, I imitated

my *No* to hear how it sounded.
I chose the pace of it, then continued

to wait in the thin reach
of darkness. The clock was enough—

and those numbers. He realized
part of the past

and left through the elm leaves.
At the curtain I heard the night

chanting. For once,
I was guilty

of nothing, not even
the moon's sprawling.

Pillows into Dark

In every shadow, I said *No*
to sleep, to that predation,
those fields of breaks.

When I finally
folded myself
into the bed, unholy
knifed my body
from its desperate
restraints, I was wake-
licked, sheet-spun
to the wall opposite.

For hours I lay
beneath the clear
rhetoric of moon
with my tired
absolutes. Imitated myself
as I said that uneven *No,*

my serrated morsel.
That answer grasped
my hips. Night:
the yank of it.

Outside, the mountains rose
and I eased
at last, before day broke
to its material. Before
it cleaned its feathers. And *No,*
I said. And I agreed.

Tongue Tender at the Center

The true true world.
Such a slim door and all
drowned desert light—oh, spine

of rib to rib to fire-
heat of summer. Soon so fast

less and less eats through the dark. I wander alone here
in the beautiful window,

awake in flags
of light
in famish. Why not sit on the white flaked wood,

eat at his elbow (again? impossible!).

Why not measure
the tangle in language and particles
of sky?

He said *sorry, sorry*
turning his eyes to sink in. The scorched place—unsolvable

with its stories lifted
out of the body and knuckled and tucked. Can I give a confession under stars
and what is it good for? A skin of absorption

keeps writing down
with a black pen the musk of pages. And after it,

camera
memory
gap: the door paused to click shut.

Renounce, or not.
Or not

to better remember and should.
Pillow-lip the animal of need. This place

without closets
has enviable skies—hardly damp, hardly coy.

Explosive.

WRONG PLACE

This morning at 10, a woman suggested I drive
to find creases of silence in low cottonwoods
thick by a river. The air was fresh then, and I thirsted
but the day had its own definition
of time, and became 1 PM when I left, and almost
an hour of driving. I was eluded by shade,
soaked to the upholstered seat. When I got
to the turn-off, I took it, unsure
of direction. A mile or two on the serpentine road,
the sun had converted to grievance
and the fire of it scraped my arms,
the back of my neck. I parked and slipped
through a hole in the tamarisk, which nodded
fringed heads toward slight mud.
Geese stayed near a few thistle
with their beaks and nostrils exact
and not higher. The river hardly fluttered:
cells of water, uninterrupted. I sat in the wreck
of illusion, pretending what I hadn't first wanted,
that stranger's idea of magnificence,
now didn't matter. Why did I need more
hush or beauty when there was enough
in the place I was staying? On the drive back,
I noticed the grand New Mexican clouds
singing with light. The road curved,
flaunting new mountains and gorges, then dipped
into valleys of cedar, chamisa
and scrub. To the west, land opened out—
steady, brown, weary, but peaceful. And the sky
by now was a giant canopy of multiple blues, sprawled
wide and lazy behind clouds suddenly flounced
with reaction. It was all about looking,
wherever I was. No time had been wasted.

To Mabel: Letter Beside the Fireplace

Do you remember that thin line Cather wrote? *You never really knew a man...until you saw him die.* Writing about suicide and miners on the plains, she was, in her simple way, turning words through yearning: *Most men were game, and went without a grudge.*

A man in your living room, as the last of day spilled out of it, knew gusts or holes, lemons or vanquish, summer breaking.

Low frequencies signal the beginning of disappointment. I hear them enough—tones with slatted pauses. That Welsh man was slipping between earth and sky when he flung those sudden mumbles of sin, the poor quivers. He argued himself into verbs and studied the back of my arm.

As you know, each loneliness offers plenty of options. After that, he showed me the contours of his winters. The death of water, death of the inner sun. Death of one's own prayer.

You've felt this. It drove you to mountains.

My voice was riddled, my pomegranate flesh aching to wake to jolts he'd write on each pane of skin. We sat under these silent windows panning our endless fractions.

Rot the memories! Especially ones like these. I think you'd say we all die and then live. I am not quite sure. Please leave me two answers.

CLEANING THE LABYRINTH

At near night, without stars,
agree to the spiral:
one breath,
then another.
Let the moon change
color. The route
is an arrangement
of organized struggles. No one
to see you tripping over.
This afternoon, long winds punished
cottonwoods, clipped heavy limbs
and flung them to maze.
Kick them aside, loving best
the next turn. To rid
the circle of flux, bend
and throw branches from the round.
(Otherwise, I am not here
with myself.) Step again to enter
and withdraw from the middle.
A labyrinth is for calming
the breach. It takes a long time
for redemption or something
similar. Stacked pebbles
embellish the dust. Walk without
thinking, steady and quiet. Hear
upraised tree limbs. Hear wind
without logic direct
one possible way.

Exposure

After Ansel Adams' *Moonrise Over Hernandez, New Mexico 1941*

Stood by the edge of the mountain, the day coming fully
to crows. Stood and the lighted gap offered a moment
of brightest compassion. Before wither, I could intercept
the warm air of distance, knew I would render it drenched
in rigorous grays. I stood in the lack and metered
to make it abundant. Clocking each crescent of moon
and its upward direction. All eye level was surface. The stars
were precise in beginning. Long was the view, though
short its duration. Cloaked at the tripod, I was entrusted
to claim province. Stood in these details: a field, a church,
desert crust, barn door. A moon, ascending, partly
undressed in devotion. My hands again moved a slide
to the holder. Saturated blue slumped over, taking its pitch,
and for a moment, peeling back, in portals of time.

PLAYBACK

Let there be footfall and car door. Let me
be finished with fire. Let
the man get on a plane for his morning
departure, erasing each reverie. Soon
there will be only daylight,
maybe a blue envelope, torn. Maybe bracelets
of color from the petunias. I will need
to know how to recover
the familiar, how to open the door
in the evening. How to again lock it.
Almost everything about me goes unspoken,
but commas and colons. I live with this
heart rate, multiple times, its direction,
its tempo: my 4/4 with acceleration, sometimes
tuned to an alternate signature. Think of Brubeck's
"Take Five." Those blocky chords were the result
of an accident—dead on arrival, they said,
after he smashed to the surf. Think how
he switched it around, made his hands
do what he wanted to hear, and forgive me
for the analogy. May I never
rush a surge for a better experience.
Every Sunday all over the country,
apologies gather. When I'm not in this
small cottage, unreacting, I cascade sound
and a few sentences from a cramped
room to whoever will listen. I know some
people believe it is sinful to love such temptations,

but I stay with my face soft against
microphone, announcing my moral
directions. Sometimes, I'm convinced my blood
needs all those crossings. I'm not after
absolution. The man I love taught me to want
without lyrics. Remember I haven't
gone anywhere. I'm in a thirsty way
sort of possessive. I shouldn't show this
side of myself. Try to remember I'm also praised
for my kindness. We each need to learn
to turn off some dreams so we can play
hours without creases.

Choosing an Archetype
for Mabel Dodge Luhan

1

Mabel was trickster and impulse
and hero. Or was she
unspooling fields
of wind? She was the sort who roused
each temptation to possible glory. Filled as she was
with opposites—every bit fair, all of her testing
last chances—what could she do but sift
for entrancement? Voracious, she kept changing
griefs into light. Bread, earth, canyon. Kept pulling fire
and multitudes from strangers.

She arrived as an infant
to a polished address already with a mind
to swerve from identical.

In years throughout Europe and dank-
bodied Manhattan, she grew to the discourse
of postures, then called further for a whole grand engine
of society, for steel
hours, more topics, every sensation.

2

As if
she were fortunate.

3

Sonorous turquoise. Wool. Elevations.

When the desert became urgent, Mabel thirsted
for war dances more plume than forbidden. Moved toward spirits

and the salvation of brief purity, the roots
of elusive heights. She carried her selves
to alluvial mesas and the wind shook as she tasted

its ranges—rough, undomestic.
Hope is the effort of opposing

the ego its widened ambitions, or so Carl Jung might have said

when they sat together by her fireplace
while the divine sky unmasked its bruising
spirals over Taos Mountain. The dark came down

with the integrity of evidence. Halfway within it,
neither would call this a desolate landscape.

4

Couldn't Jung see how narrow
each category is? Of course Mabel trembled
at life's inventory. (We all do.)
But she cherished the volatile
and each wedge of error
as perpetual as those wind-wracked
branches. She was the sun
gnawing a hole in a land where she crowded
her wishes. Why pick—magician, seeker or rebel—
when the possibilities are rooms
open to company? Mabel took the earth
and the size of the future.
Kept her limitations
like bones or hymns.

5

Over years of occasions
Mabel pushed to the greedy, its treasures.

So much we'll never know of the savage grasp,
but she trusted the unconscious its tremendous dreaming.

She was willing to offer it lodging.
She took in its gypsies.

Better than roosting with her shadow
as breeze conjured the hips
of the cottonwood, dodged the stream.

6

Each night Mabel must have rewound slow conversations
reckoned in her living room
as a guard against the malice of silence.

She knew she needed protection.

The Fine Mist
of Buzzing

SHADOW

Until now, I've forgotten
about the dandelion seedheads
ready to spill. Get on

with the ongoing. There is always
direction. This morning, the choke-
cherry could not proffer

a new red. On the road
four roans
by the fence, one with a stripe full

down his face. Dark
into light—the imperative—
or at least that's what I think

I extracted:
heavy shadows and stillness.
No more Mister

who walked me through night to the squat
mournful cottage. I had no hunger
for his deliberate confusion.

The design of my *no*
has turned human inside me,
my body clasped by multiple responses.

Sun pulls up.
I start to remember
why I came

through weeping trees
to where the valley emerges.
This house is all door and table. No other reason.

TODAY AND OTHER FLOWERS

Today I sat with a woman who thinks without future.
Her house holds first and last things.
In a bowl, globes of grape, pale as elm leaves;
in another, a scatter of nuts that don't touch.
She eats like a prophet—first one, then the other.
Once she painted the undulant: threshed fields,
the thickening river two miles off.
Her brushes discovered the inside of landscape.
Now her skin's gone thin and violet, and her eyes hold caves.
She doesn't know me. What she doesn't know
isn't tragic. She's fallen through,
but her hands want to be moving. She sits
in her crowded house with her German shepherds.
She sits in her blue pants with a cane
by her side. Through the many tall windows,
she sees a sky drowning in blue.
Sees pines wrinkled in heat. It is afternoon
and still is. Afternoon daisies.
From her I learn the koan of looking.
Open-throated Southwest pots—buff,
white and black—cluster in the kitchen.
She asks me a question studded with ending
and beginning; she's concentrating.
No deviation in the sheen of her thoughts.
She asks and repeats her question with the logic
of what's not important, with pieces
of asking. She's lived here for decades.
The days drift through her, and bloom into night.

She asks again where I'm going.
To the unfolding water, I tell her.
Her soft hands play with a purple pencil.
She does not latch her thoughts; she looks out
at the interior wall of the sky, the endless
distance. Together, we notice the birds that fly
to the feeder, their silent conversations
as they work on seed shells. This is why
we have shadow and yellow, why red-winged blackbirds,
why we have windows, why trees knot
at the river, and why the river turns around,
suddenly deciding to run off again
wherever its memory pleases.

LETTER TO MABEL: THE GAZE OF LAYERS

What is one supposed to say to a stranger? My heart keeps turning
the soot and the remnants. I was sealed into her morning.

You might have found the painter extraordinary, her bodies of color that
extended this spine of desert. In her hands, leftover stubble of oil, the
rusts and glimmers moist and beaming.

But tough women arrow into each other. Neither of you would have seen
the other as a friend. Never mind: You each need your mountains.

That table I sat at is every table in this small town. We sat without
ambiguities. After a while she offered slow-threaded answers. I looked
straight at the small bowls of them, the smooth, oblique centers. Collars,
blue wool, a door to a basement; we sat between spins of a fan.

To discover, one must postpone understanding. Affix space to the day
lowering around. I waited and waited. The sky went on, clouds clumping
on junipers. It was a lovely table—dark wood and almost as grand as the
one in your kitchen.

Aren't we all ghosts, overhearing the cracks in our cups? The sky was
filled with stems and limbs, the shapes complete, then missing. She and I
looked out. The thrilled whistle of the magpies! We had no more purpose
than the strands of their spell.

FOUR STREETS FROM TOWN

When there is wind in heaven I stroll through sky scars
to fertile music and the notes fall into a well like pasts or requests

On my way back to the cottage in the dark snake of night I measure time
by the last diagram of slight streets as shadows swan the chromite sky

Just before I get there my mind browses shrinking stars
and finds pleasure in thistle at the corner their blue heads loosed

I say to no one in particular I know the lines of love I am standing
in them I am softened by this vulnerable body these footsteps

Figuring out this exact substance the fold of slow wind
more and more wherever there is ambiguity I will wear it

Note to a Man in Wales with Remorse

When we talk about failure, I know
there's a daughter, a son, a banner of damp
hills and each door to a farmhouse
well-proportioned. I already know that is just
as you like it. Outside, I can hear
the trees creaking as they rest on the roof
in the wind. You might say they *lie*
on the roof, from Old English, *licgan*,
and then I think you may not say *roof*,
so I Google it up and find instead
why do British say bloody and remember
your mouth. Your face sticks
in my memory. Here I stay hidden
in this tiny house, a *hovel* you called it,
and I still keep it elaborately empty
with its rapture of light. I wonder if you
noticed that, and how is your vision?
Did you see that the bed stayed to itself
beyond doorways when you leaned in close
with your elbows? I didn't yield, and I liked
that I wouldn't give affection to the half-
cornered evening, to an almost
stranger. My capacious self with honey
on my tongue, I talked twice as little in minutes,
but how would you know? I could have
traded the full for the detail, but I made
a choice, and then stayed awake—trying
to figure out which I do, lie or lay,
or both, when I'm turned around—

as you made me. As it happens,
when you left, I went to my bed, and the body
of moon lay beside me, pulsing. I tell you
I saw it. I rose, and stroked it,
though all I could touch was the brim
and puff just developing. No, I'm not lying.
I was wearing only my necklace
of delicate language, only the room,
my arms, every hesitation, and I hardly knew
how to silence this body.

LETTER TO MABEL: RIGHT NOW, WITHOUT

By mid-afternoon, the sun is polite, conciliatory. I am falling asleep, full of the elusion, elision of his voice, flown away. I meant only to exchange landscape.

Why not let him be many others? I am in the cottage on your grounds, but apart from the Big House, your stones. Swallow, erase, regret, censor. There is every flung light over acre. At the bottom of thought, I begin to rebuild the slender flames of my attention.

It is Thursday or Sunday, or any indication of a day that returns to itself. He has left, and it is the first day.

MY BED IN THE LUMINOUS FRAY

Last night the moon took me back
in its discipline
as if light could restore what I'd carefully set aside.
The window flickered its lace.

I leaned on my white pillow,
with the white sheet across the map of my body.
The luminous peered through
in eddies and settled its fine blooms.

Last night, the moon was plump.
My bed ridden by lightness.

AND SOMEHOW MORE LIGHT

Next to the chokecherry, the wooden rail,
and steps up to the larger house. The summer
is already poured into a chair. A night and another
without anyone important, nothing to mention,
then a morning, springy around me. Auden once
wrote of suffering in art, that it exists,
but not all of us notice. After the last exhibit I saw,
the paintings followed me everywhere,
those oil-on-canvas deep gazes and details
and thick rippled colors. And when I entered
the day again, pushed the double doors open,
multiple layers and splashes of orange
played on the sky, which had soft scumbled
edges. I loved the particular gleam of horizon
and new gasps of my vision—unlike that flat
afternoon I left home. Which is, in a way,
what he was discussing. Auden, I mean,
in his poem, and I'm stretching the metaphor a little,
lingering on the most brilliant colors, but
the prerogative of desire is distance and choosing
what you'll look at. So what if sometimes
it's the incarnadine, seductive? Once I went
with my father to see a room of Rothkos
at the Philadelphia Museum of Art. My dad couldn't
handle his boredom. All those boxes. I stood
in front of them, crushed, for long minutes.

There were no edges! no innocence! The critics
argue whether the artist's later works
were tragic, but there was something miraculous
happening—and that day, I couldn't
let it resolve without me. Parallel variations;
sometimes you need them. As a girl, I collected
fireflies on hot summer evenings, running
around the backyard with a glass
jar, mouth open. Inside, the flies turned off
their continuous light. They silenced
their prism. Back then, I didn't understand
loss or drifting, but now in the long arc
of summer, if I sit outside, a beer in one hand,
the trees will keep falling above me,
loosing their cotton, and insects will recklessly,
perilously quiver. I know I can't capture them.
Wind comes in from the cemetery and park.
The sound of buzzing. Such thrilling lanterns.

PEOPLE IN FRONT OF ME

I've read what I can find and walked through the park.
What I know is all but the haunt of her voice.
I want to love her palest thoughts. An arrow,
a brief significance, she was desperate
to arrive on the other side of fences. The magpies never stop
sniffing and chucking their targets, clustered. Mabel, dead-
serious in every picture, apprehensive
of solitude. You could say she built a last resort

but despite hitching her name the third time to "primitive"
was given only a carved, latched
wooden door and rooms that cross high and low.
In this borrowed cottage, away from the harm
of an earth left to dry, I sleep with measureless gasps.
Doesn't matter whether full moon or shredded.

I'm convinced the fault of her thoughts
was born of her infinite obstinate sadness.
Always two miles ahead, the blooming
broad cactus. Around a curve, a bridge levied
by trusses. Everywhere I look, distance sweeps on
with the maximum extraction of horizon.
I'm thinking about where I live, a hundred miles down.
Every week people cry in front of me. Near strangers

emptying their stories, and the common brain wants
its intersections, so I enter each frame of their widening narratives.
But here, I'm presumably alone.
From this compact cottage I trail off, desire
nothing. Maybe pliable ground.
I notice the sky is waiting to find its behaviors. I pass a black cross

then reach the *morada*, thick-bodied.
Through neglected windows light falls plural
with dutiful spirits on empty interiors. What good
is wanting? Mabel claimed the village, calling it self, clawing
it to her to startle her consequence. I know nothing more
than aftermath. Tomorrow I still won't
be sleeping at home. Bearskin and vigas, uncurtained
windows. Stones at her threshold took over the ruts.

What appears is an entire field
of eyes. They start and displace. Does it matter
whether mourners or hopefuls? House to house, those eyes
are ours. The magpies are thundering
and Mabel is home. Here is a mountain. Need nothing else.

To Account for the End

Where I live, everyone I know is divining
for rain, for new shadows—as a man might open
the thighs of a woman, expecting

the heart between hills, the muggy pleasures.
It has been sunny for a year and eighteen
before that. I drove into the mountains to get away

from my rearview mirror. Soon, the faint scent of artists took over. Soon,

the faint scent of artists with their fleshes
and brushes will be previous. Soon, even the ground

that seemed carnal will be only
flat, only twice felt. Soon, my last night
of trees. All these sentences that took so terribly long
to accumulate. These will remember.

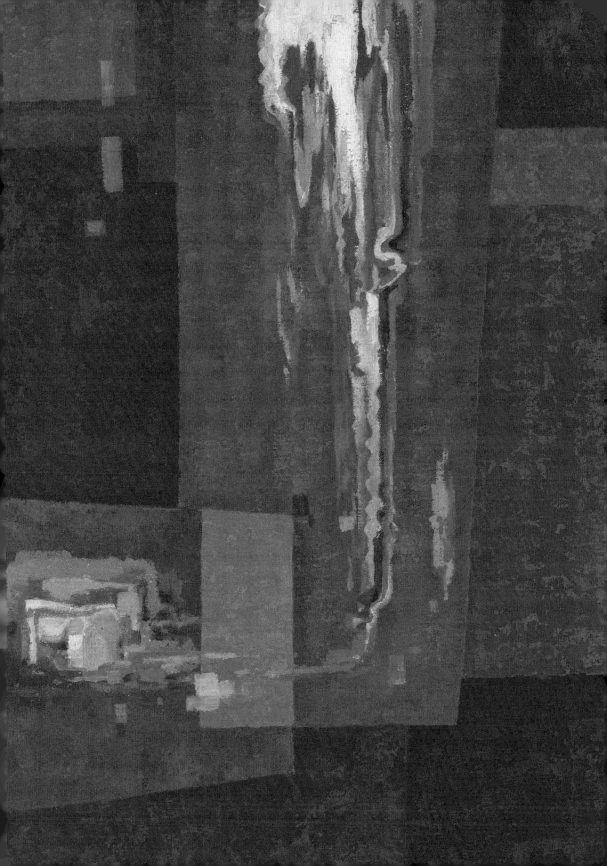

Letter to Mabel: On the Crescent of Home

As I left, the ditch was full but not running. A swallowtail flew over my head within inches. A fragrance of light, something to feed me.

I turned from your home where I let go the interrogation of ash. Entered the script of oak and aspen. Every worry taken from me. And now to the roads and folds and tender way down. There is gold in the sky, on the trees—continuous and distant. The sparks are as fists, and I am about to return to their constriction. Is this on my heart? Is anything?

I drive. I know the way: *First pass the white gate, then the rusted red one.*

— **Our Beginning and Our End**

In the languages of the various pueblos, places were named by natural characteristics. Driving north from Santa Fe (named *'ogap'oge* in Tewa for the olivella, which was used to make shell money), you pass three villages included in the poem: Tesuque (in Tewa, *tecuge*) or "dry spotted place;" Pojoaque (in Tewa, *posuwaegeh*) or "drink water place;" and Cuyamungue (*k'uyemuge*), noted for "where people hurled stones," as defense during ancient times of warfare. One of the Tiwa names for Taos derived from its red willow trees. (Harrington, 353, 355, 357).

— **The House of What We Invent**

Arts patron Mabel Dodge Luhan began building the house in Taos in 1918 and hosted visitors there until 1929. Many had been part of the social and intellectual gatherings ("salons") at her Greenwich Village home. Mabel's plan was to combine the primitive experience she found in Taos with the social and political energy she created in the more cosmopolitan places she had lived.

Lincoln Steffens, Progressive era muckraker, told Mabel, "You have a certain faculty, a centralizing, magnetic, social faculty. You attract, stimulate, and soothe people, and men like to sit with you and talk to themselves! You make them think more fluently and they feel enhanced...Now why don't you see what you can do with this gift of yours? Why not organize all this accidental, unplanned activity around you? This coming and going of visitors, and see these people at certain hours? Have Evenings!" (Wetzsteon, 16-7).

Many influential creative thinkers and scholars—including Marsden Hartley, Martha Graham, Ansel Adams, Willa Cather, Robinson Jeffers, Georgia O'Keeffe, D. H. Lawrence, and Frank Waters—spent time in her Big House in Taos.

— **Rainbow Room and the Red Chair**

Mabel handwrote her memoirs in the Rainbow Room of the Big House, beneath wooden beams which she had painted to resemble an Indian blanket. I wrote most of *Turquoise Door* in that same room.

— **Feathers and Mountain**

Tony Lujan was Mabel's fourth husband and an enrolled member of the Taos Pueblo. One story asserts that he painted birds throughout the upstairs of the Big House he and Mabel built in Taos.

— The Sighing of the Kit Carson Cemetery
Mabel Dodge Luhan is buried in this cemetery in Taos.

— Willa Cather at the Big House
The quotation is from Cather's *Death Comes for the Archbishop*.

— Vanishing Point
E. (Eanger) Irving Couse was one of the founding members of the Taos Society of Artists, which flourished from 1915 to 1927. As Virginia Leavitt at The Couse-Sharp Historic Site taught me, Eanger is pronounced like *angel*, but with an R at the end.

— Temple of Lawrence
The italic phrases are drawn from D. H. Lawrence's novels, *Kangaroo* and *Lady Chatterley's Lover.*

Lawrence and his wife Frieda first visited Taos on invitation from Mabel. They arrived on September 11, 1922, Lawrence's 37th birthday. He wrote of his first impressions of Taos shortly after, "In the magnificent fierce morning of New Mexico, one sprang awake, a new part of the soul woke up suddenly and the old world gave way to the new."

Mabel gifted the Lawrence couple with a 160-acre ranch twenty miles north of Taos, in San Cristóbal, New Mexico. In return, Frieda gave Mabel the original manuscript of *Sons and Lovers*.

Lawrence spent a total of 11 months on the ranch (between 1923 and 1925). This was the only time he lived in America and the only property he ever owned. He died of tuberculosis in Venice on March 1, 1930, but Frieda had his body exhumed and cremated, and the ashes are now housed in a one-room shrine on the ranch.

— Letter to Mabel: From a Door Turning Inward
Near the front door of the D. H. Lawrence ranch, there is a grand Ponderosa pine. Lawrence often sat below it, on a wooden bench, to write in the mornings. The tree also caught Georgia O'Keeffe's interest. She was at the ranch five years after Lawrence's final visit. She painted *The Lawrence Tree* (1929) from the perspective of lying on the bench and looking up into the vast limbs of the tree.

— Green Lesson

This poem is for Georgia O'Keeffe, another of Mabel's visitors.

— The Agnes Martins at the Harwood Museum

The Harwood Museum of Art in Taos has a permanent gallery devoted to work by abstractionist and long-time resident, Agnes Martin. The meditative space holds seven of her 5' X 5', blue and white paintings: "Lovely Life," "Love," "Friendship," "Perfect Day," "Ordinary Happiness," "Innocence," and "Playing."

— Plucking the Lake from Devotion

In 1906, the sacred Blue Lake of the Taos Pueblo was appropriated by the U.S. Government and placed under control of the United States Forest Service. After 64 years of protest by tribal members, on December 15, 1970, then President Richard M. Nixon signed Public Law 91-550. Nixon stated, "This is a bill that represents justice, because in 1906 an injustice was done in which land involved in this bill, 48,000 acres, was taken from...the Taos Pueblo Indians. The Congress of the United States now returns that land to whom it belongs... ."

The eagle plumes are part of the legend of the origin of the Taos Pueblo. (Miller, p.15).

— Lucero Peak Cave

D. H. Lawrence's short story, "The Woman Who Rode Away," was inspired by a visit he made to the cave with Mabel in 1922. She writes about it in *Lorenzo in Taos*. Reading this story led me to the cave—and this poem.

— And Somehow More Light

This poem references W.H. Auden's "Musée des Beaux Arts."

— Choosing an Archetype for Mabel Dodge Luhan

Carl Jung visited Taos when Mabel was in New York. The two never met, and he never stayed at her house, but I wondered which of his archetypes he would have chosen for Mabel. At first, I thought "trickster"—unconscious shadow, mercurial, undaunted by failure, exceptional appetites—but changed my mind as I wrote the poem.

— To Mabel: Letter Beside the Fireplace

This poem references Willa Cather's *My Antonia*, a critically acclaimed book that Mabel likely read. Cather was a visitor to the Mabel Dodge Luhan House in the summers of 1925 and 1926.

— People in Front of Me

La Morada de Nuestra Señora de Guadalupe (the Taos Morada) is one of the most sacred holy sites in the area. It was built between 1810 and 1830 to serve La Fraternidad Piadosa de Nuestro Padre Jesús Nazareno (the pious organization also known as the Penitente brotherhood or *penitentes*) for their lay religious practice and devotion. The morada is not currently in use. (Nathanson).

— Exposure

I wanted to capture Ansel Adams' signature style of long-exposure landscape photography with a poem based on his image made in northern New Mexico. Adams shot *Moonrise Over Hernandez, New Mexico 1941* while on assignment for the Department of the Interior. His task was to take photographs of the U.S. landscape. Adams visited the Mabel Dodge Luhan House in 1927, 1929 and 1930.

BIBLIOGRAPHY

Adams, Ansel. *Examples: The Making of 40 Photographs*.
(Boston: Little, Brown, 1989). Print.

Allan, Rebecca. "Mabel Dodge Luhan: A Force of Nature for Art." *Fine Art Connoisseur*
(May/June 2016). Print.

Brown, Patricia Leigh. "The Muse of Taos, Stirring Still." *The New York Times*
(January 16, 1997). Print.

Burke, Flannery. *From Greenwich Village to Taos: Primitivism and Place at
Mabel Dodge Luhan's*.
(Lawrence, Kan.: U of Kansas, 2008). Print.

Cather, Willa. *Death Comes for the Archbishop*.
(New York: A.A. Knopf, 1927). Print.

Cunningham, Elizabeth. *Remarkable Women of Taos*.
(Taos: Nighthawk Press, 2013). Print.

Dyer, Geoff. *Out of Sheer Rage: Wrestling with D. H. Lawrence*.
(New York: North Point, 1998). Print.

Dzelzitis, Roz. *History of the Conflict*.
Sacred Land Film Project, Taos Blue Lake. N.p., Web. (June, 2002).

Harrington, John Peabody. *Old Indian Geographical Names around Santa Fe, New Mexico*.
(Washington, D.C.: *American Anthropologist*, 22.4, 1920). Web.

Keegan, Marcia. *The Taos Indians and Their Sacred Blue Lake*.
(New York: J. Messner, 1972). Print.

Lawrence, D. H. *Kangaroo*.
(New York: Viking, 1960). Print.

Lawrence, D. H. *Lady Chatterley's Lover.*
(New York: Grove, 1957). Print.

Luhan, Mabel Dodge. *Edge of Taos Desert.*
(New York: Harcourt, Brace, 1937). Print.

Luhan, Mabel Dodge. *Lorenzo in Taos.*
(New York: Knopf, 1932). Print.

Miller, Page Putnam. *Landmarks of American Women's History*.
(Oxford: Oxford UP, 2003). Print.

Nathanson, Rick. "Updated: Taos' History, Allure Linked to Personalities Who Have Called It Home." *Albuquerque Journal.*
(N.p., n.d. Web. 13 Dec. 2016.)

Rudnick, Lois Palken, and MaLin Wilson-Powell. *Mabel Dodge Luhan & Company: American Moderns and the West.*
(Santa Fe: Museum of New Mexico, 2016). Print.

Wetzsteon, Ross. *Republic of Dreams: Greenwich Village, the American Bohemia,* 1910-1960.
(N.p.: Simon & Schuster, 2003). Print.

Acknowledgments

The author wishes to acknowledge the editors of the following publications in which these poems first appeared, some in different forms or with different titles:

About Place Journal — "Dear Mabel"

Belmont Story Review — "Icon"

BOAAT — "First Longing"

Cider Press Review — "Note to a Man in Wales with Remorse"

Compose — "Dear One Who Stays"

Crannóg — "Cleaning the Labyrinth"

Crazyhorse — "Our Beginning and Our End"

Cutthroat — "Willa Cather at the Big House"

decomP — "Letter to Mabel: Lingering in the Corner"

Diode — "And Somehow More Light"

DoveTales — "Summer Drifting in Shy Talk"

Driftless Review — "Here, and Here"

El Palacio — "The Sighing of the Kit Carson Cemetery," "Temple of Lawrence,"
      "The Half Measure to Pleasure and Places," and "Feathers and Mountain"

[Ex]tinguished & [Ex]tinct Anthology (Twelve Winters Press) — "Pinwheeled *Descansos*"

Fixed and Free Poetry Anthology — "Hour of the Turning Moon"

ISLE: Interdisciplinary Studies in Literature and Environment — "Wrong Place" and
      "Last Stain of June Sun"

Lumen — "The First to Refuse"

New Madrid — "First Rain in Eight Months"

Nimrod International Journal — "Letter to Mabel: Under Vigas"

Poem-a-Day (Academy of American Poets) — "Playback"

Posit — "God of the Clustered Night"

RHINO — "Today and Other Flowers"

Slice — "To Account for the End"

South Dakota Review — "Choosing an Archetype for
      Mabel Dodge Luhan"

Spillway — "Past Tense"

String Poet — "To Wake at the Point of All Sleeping"

Taos Journal of International Poetry & Art — "Pillows into Dark"

The Asheville Poetry Review — "What Needed Saying"

The Fourth River — "Canyon Trail #59"

THE Magazine — "The Agnes Martins at the Harwood Museum"

The Poetry Mail — "Awake All Night. Not"

Third Coast — "People in Front of Me"

Tinderbox Poetry Journal — "My Bed in the Luminous Fray"

Waccamaw — "Lucero Peak Cave"

Weaving the Terrain: 100-Word Southwestern Poems (Dos Gatos Press, 2018) —
    "Letter to Mabel: Right Now, Without"

Zócalo Public Square — "Exposure"

"Pinwheeled *Descansos*" was reprinted in OCELLI.

"Canyon Trail #59" was reprinted in the Riverfeet Press Anthology (2017).

In Appreciation

This book began when I first stepped into The Mabel Dodge Luhan House, in Taos, New Mexico, for an extended stay as Poet-in-Residence. Very quickly, I wanted to understand Mabel's complicated history and to interact with the artists she brought to this desert outpost a century ago. I thank the staff at Mabel's house for the opportunity to be there.

Thank you, thank you to Andrea Watson and 3: A Taos Press for believing in this book.

Appreciation to D. H. Lawrence Ranch groundskeeper Ricardo Medina for taking me to the cabins and the shrine and to Kristin Peterson at Hotel La Fonda de Taos for unveiling the Forbidden D. H. Lawrence paintings. Thanks, too, to Virginia and Ernie Leavitt at The Couse-Sharp Historic Site for sharing the studios and history of E.I. Couse and J.H. Sharp, and in so doing, for piquing my interest in the Taos Society of Artists.

Thanks to *El Palacio*, the magazine for the Museums of New Mexico, for showcasing four of these poems early on in the writing of this book.

And my love to David, who chooses to go backward and forward in history with me every day and night.

ABOUT THE AUTHOR

Lauren Camp is the author of three previous books, including *One Hundred Hungers*, which won the Dorset Prize and was a finalist for the Arab American Book Award, the Sheila Margaret Motton Award, and the Housatonic Book Award. Her poems have appeared in *Slice, Ecotone, Boston Review, Beloit Poetry Journal* and the Poem-a-Day series from The Academy of American Poets. A Black Earth Institute Fellow, Lauren lives and teaches in New Mexico.

Also by 3: A Taos Press

Collecting Life: Poets on Objects Known and Imagined – Madelyn Garner and Andrea Watson

Seven – Sheryl Luna

The Luminosity – Bonnie Rose Marcus

Trembling in the Bones: A Commemorative Edition – Eleanor Swanson

3 A.M. – Phyllis Hotch

Ears of Corn: Listen – Max Early

Elemental – Bill Brown

Rootwork – Veronica Golos

Farolito – Karen S. Córdova

Godwit – Eva Hooker

The Ledgerbook – William S. Barnes

The Mistress – Catherine Strisik

Library of Small Happiness – Leslie Ullman

Day of Clean Brightness – Jane Lin

Bloodline – Radha Marcum

Hum of Our Blood – Madelyn Garner

Dark Ladies & Other Avatars – Joan Roberta Ryan

The Doctor of Flowers – Rachel Blum

Bird Forgiveness – Melinda Palacio